CONTENTS

Foreword 2
Geography Glossary A-Z 3
Index 50

HOW TO USE THIS BOOK

You will see geography vocabulary in **bold** throughout this book. For example:

A **marsh** is a type of **wetland**.

Every **bold** word appears in the <u>index</u> of this book. To understand the word **marsh**, you will need to understand what a **wetland** is, both of which is in this glossary! Just search in the index if you are not sure of something and there you will see which page you can find the definition.

Visit us at www.bclesterbooks.com for more!

No part of this book may be copied, reproduced or sold without express permission from the copyright owner.

Copyright B.C. Lester Books 2021. All rights reserved.

A QUICK MESSAGE FROM US

Hey! Thank you for making the purchase, we really hope you enjoy this book. If you have the chance, then all feedback is greatly appreciated. We have put a lot of effort into making this book, so if you are not completely satisfied, please email us at ben@bclesterbooks.com and we will do our best to address the issues. If you have any suggestions, enquiries or want to send us a selfie with this book, then email at the same address - ben@bclesterbooks.com

Is this book misprinted? Drop us an email with a photo of the misprint and we will send out another copy!

WHO ARE WE AT B.C LESTER BOOKS?

B.C. Lester Books is a publishing firm based in Buckinghamshire, UK. With our passion and how-know for geography, we aim to provide quality works based around the topic. We have already released a selection of activity, trivia and fact books for kids and adults and are working hard to bring you wider selection. Have a suggestion for us? Then drop us an email! We are all ears!

HAVE FUN WITH OUR GIFT TO YOU: A 3-IN-1 GEOGRAPHY QUIZ BOOK
(AND GET ACCESS TO MORE GEOGRAPHY MATERIAL FOR KIDS)

Go here to grab your FREE copy!
www.bclesterbooks.com/freebies

ARCH

An *arch (or sea arch – and specifically a natural arch)* is a rock formation shaped as an arch. They commonly form from the erosion of **cliffs** or **stacks**.

A **stack (or seastack)** is a steep and vertical column of rock in the sea near the **coast**. They form from the erosion of **cliffs** or **arches**.

ARCHIPELAGO

An *archipelago* is a chain, cluster or group of **islands**. Examples include the Hawaiian islands, which is a chain, and the Bahamas, which is a group.

The Hawaiian Islands archipelago

Credit: NASA

BAY

A *bay* is an inlet of the **ocean** where the land curves inwards. A large *bay* is also called a **gulf** or even a **sea**. A large *bay* that is shallow and only bend a little is called a **bight**. A small *bay* with a small entrance and round shape is also called a **cove**. A small, narrow and long *bay* is called an **inlet**.

BEACH

A *beach* is a strip of land appearing at the boundary between land and bodies of water such as an **ocean** or **lake**. A *beach* is made up of particles such as sand, pebbles or shells. A *beach* is found at a **shore** and at a **coast**.

A **shore (or shoreline)** is the area that forms the boundary between land and a large body of water. The **shore** is an area between the water's edge and the extent of the **ocean's** action (high tide) inland. A **coast (also coastline, seashore)** is a **shore** that must border an **ocean**.

BIOME

A *biome* is a region with shared plants and animals that have been shaped by the environment they are in. Examples include **deserts**, **tundra**, **grassland** and **taiga**.

▲ BUTTE

A *butte* is an isolated **hill** with steep sides and a small, flat top. A **knoll** or **hillock** is also an isolated hill, similar in size to a *butte* but without the steep sides.

A **mesa** is a larger version of a *butte*, typically with a flat top longer than it's vertical height. A **mesa** features a **plateau** and is surrounded by a steep **cliff** called an **escarpment**.

Buttes and **mesas** form from erosion and are found in **badlands biomes**. **Badlands** are areas with heavily eroded **landforms** and low vegetation.

CANYON

A *canyon* is a deep **valley** between **cliff** faces. Canyons are formed by the erosive activity of **rivers** over long periods of time. A **gorge** is similar to a *canyon* but often narrower and smaller. A **ravine** is another similar term, but ravines are narrower and smaller than *canyons*. A **gully** resembles a *canyon*, but on a much smaller scale, being formed by the erosion on soil rather than rock.

CAVE

A *cave (also called cavern)* is an opening in the ground that is big enough for human entry. Interesting rock formations may be found inside a *cave*, all resulting from years of mineral (rock forming) deposits. The three most common ones being a **column** (1), **stalactite** (2) and **stalagmite** (3)!

CHANNEL

A *channel* is a narrow and shallow body of water that generally describes **rivers**, **deltas** and **straits**. A **strait** is a narrow waterway connecting two larger bodies of water, and may be thought of as the water version of an **isthmus**. A **canal** is an artificial waterway or *channel* used in water transport.

▲ The English Channel. The narrowest point in this *channel* is called the Strait Of Dover.

CLIFF

A *cliff* (also bluff) is a vertical (or nearly vertical) rock faced **landform**. *Cliffs* are often found on the border between land and **ocean** (on the **coast**). *Cliffs* may also appear in **mountainous** areas and alongside **rivers**. *Cliffs* are formed by the processes of erosion and weathering.

◀ CONTINENT

A *continent* is a large landmass. These are Africa, Antarctica (on the **south pole**), Asia, Australia & Oceania, Europe, North America and South America. These *continents* make up the landmass of **Earth**.

▲ DELTA

A *delta* (or river delta) is land created by the deposition of sediment where a **river** flows into a body of water such as an **ocean**, **sea** or **lake**. *Deltas* form when the **river** gets too weak to continue to transport sediment. As a result, the *delta* forces the **river** to split into multiple **channels** called **distributaries**.

DEPRESSION

A *depression* is land that is sunk below the surrounding area. Depressions may be formed in diverse ways. A **basin** is a type of *depression* normally formed from tectonic activity. A **valley** is a type of *depression* formed from erosion. A **caldera** is a *depression* that forms after the emptying of a **magma chamber**. A **sinkhole** is a *depression* formed when rocks collapse into an underground hollow.

DESERT

A *desert* is a biome with low rainfall, resulting in minimal vegatation and minimal animal life. *Deserts* form with weathering processes such as the breaking of rocks from temperature differences between day and night. *Deserts* may be hot, such as the Sahara Desert, but also may be cold, such as Antarctica, which is known as a **polar desert**. In *deserts,* sand may form **hills** or **ridges** called a **dune**. If an underground water source surfaces in a *desert*, this creates an **oasis**.

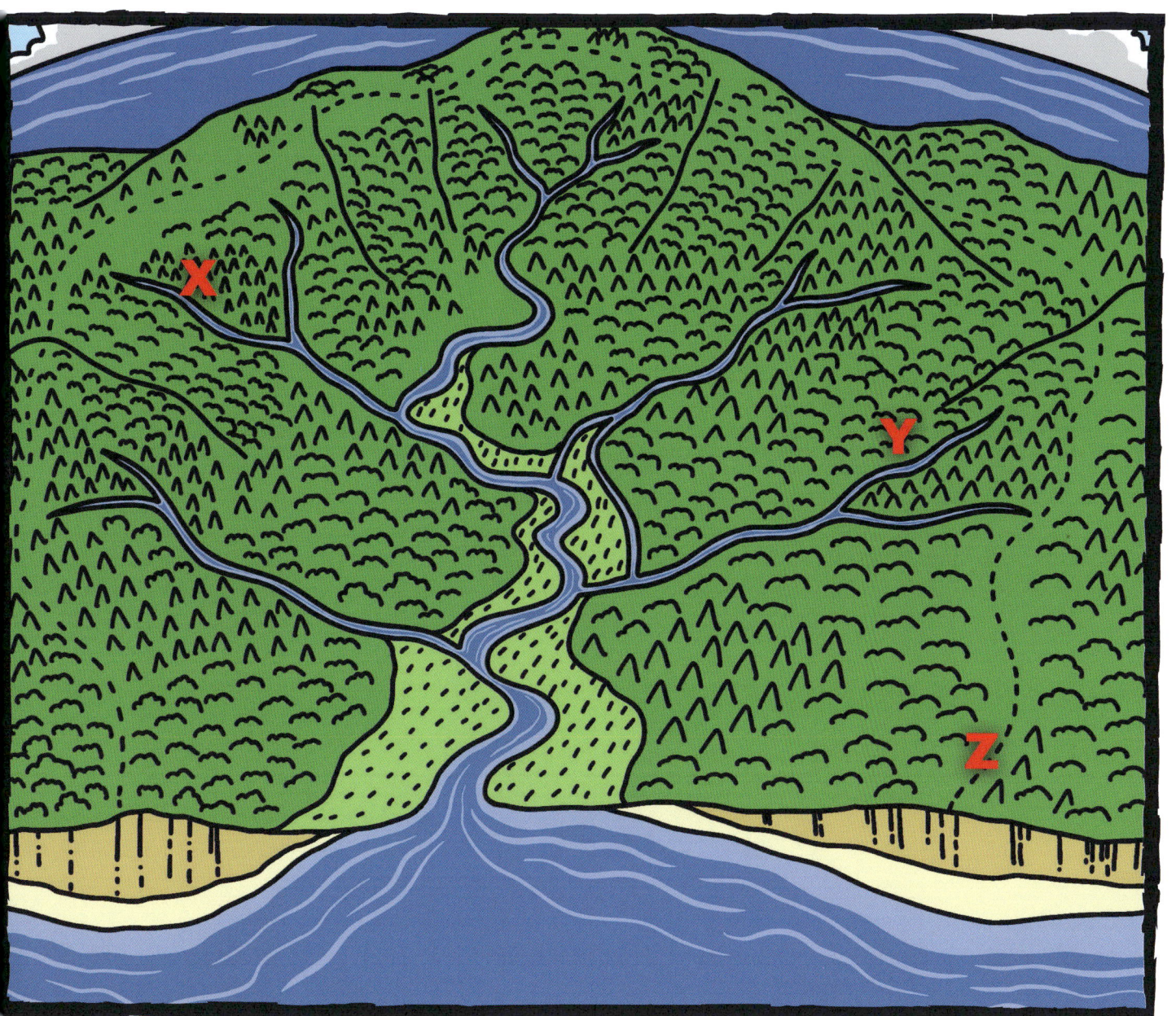

DRAINAGE BASIN

A *drainage basin (also called the watershed in the USA)* is an area of land where rain and other precipitation drain into a common outlet such as a **river**. As you can see, rain in places **X** and **Y** will drain downhill and will end in the same main **river** through smaller, connected **rivers** and **streams** called **tributaries**. The boundary of the *drainage basin* is called a **drainage divide** (also *watershed* outside the USA, see the dashed line, **Z**). Outside the **drainage divide**, rainfall flows into different outlets.

A **tributary** (also called **affluent**) is a **river** or **stream** that flows into a larger **river**. The point where a **tributary** joins a larger **river** is called a **confluence**. Almost all rivers will have **tributaries**, and the collective network of **river** and its **tributaries** form the *drainage basin*.

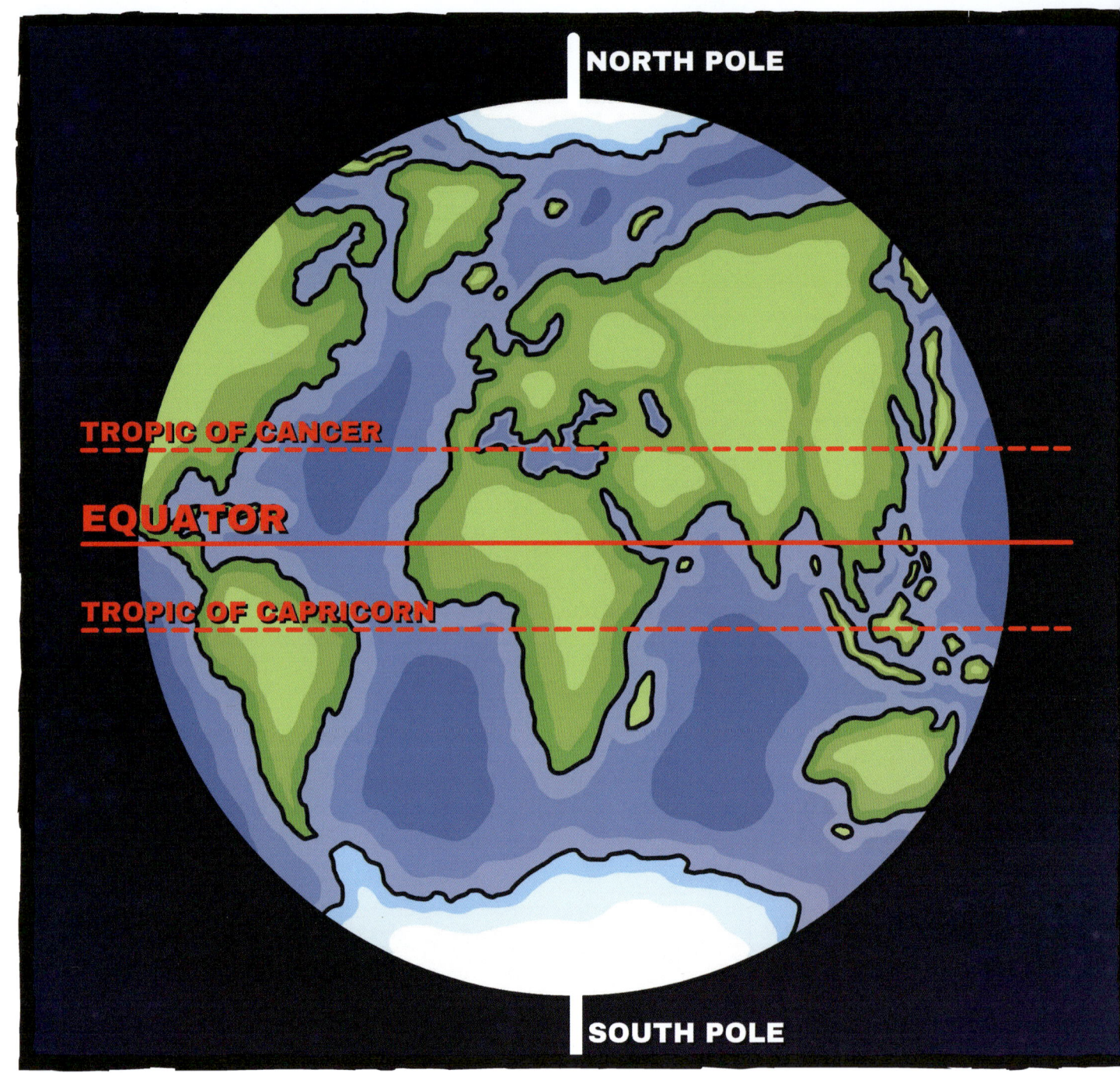

EARTH

Earth is the planet we live on, and it's spherical model is called a **globe**. The **equator** separates *Earth* into a northern half and southern half. The *Earth* rotates on an axis that is tilted by 23.5 degrees. The ends of the axis form the **North Pole** and **South Pole**. That means that the 2 lines, the **Tropic Of Cancer** - sitting 23.5 degrees above the **equator** - and the **Tropic Of Capricorn** - sitting 23.5 degrees below the **equator** - mark the maximum extent of this tilt. The **Tropic Of Cancer** is the most northerly place that may be the closest to the sun at any point, and similarly, the **Tropic Of Capricorn** is the most southerly place for this.

ESTUARY

An *estuary* is a partially enclosed body of water with a **river** or **stream** flowing into it and a connection to a **sea** or **ocean**. *Estuaries* are a transitional zone between a **river** or **stream**, and an **ocean** and are therefore less salty than seawater but more salty than freshwater. An *estuary* follows the **ocean's** tide, but also carries flows from the **river**. An *estuary* is similar to a **bay**, **ria** and **lagoon**.

▲ FIORD

A *fiord (also spelt fjord)* is a long, narrow **bay** surrounded by **cliffs** or steep sides. A *fiord* is created by the erosion of a **glacier**. A **sound** is less narrow and has less steep sides than a *fiord*.

▲ FOREST

A *forest* is an area of land dominated by trees. This means that the trees here are dense and they cover large areas. A **woodland** (or woods) is a similar term that also is an area dominated by trees but refers to smaller areas than *forests*. There are several types of *forest* such as **boreal (taiga)**, coniferous, deciduous and **rainforests**.

GEYSER

A *geyser* is a **spring** that discharges hot water from time to time. Geysers form as a result of underground water stores being heated up by it's location close to **magma**. Once hot enough, the pressurised water and steam vents out.

GLACIER

A *glacier* is persistent ice that is moving under its own weight, being forced downhill by gravity. *Glaciers* may appear in polar regions as **ice sheets,** such as in Antarctica, or in **mountainous** regions. Because of their large weight, the movement causes glacial ice to come under stress, creating deep cracks called **crevasses.** *Glaciers* are able to transport and deposit rocks, creating areas scattered with rocks called **moraines**.

If large chunks of ice break off from the *glacier* and end up in the **ocean**, these chunks of ice are called **icebergs**.

GRASSLAND

A *grassland* is an area dominated by grasses. It forms a major **biome** on **Earth**. Major types of grassland include **savanna**, **steppe** and meadows.

HILL ▲

A *hill* is land that rises above the surrounding terrain. A *hill* is less steep and less tall than a **mountain**. A hill has a **summit**.

ISLAND

An *island* (or *isle*) is a body of land that is completely surrounded by water. An *island* must also be a landmass that is not a **continent**; meaning that Australia, despite it looking like an *island* on a world map, is not actually one. An **islet** is a very small *island*. A **key** or **cay** is a very small and flat *island* that is on the surface of a **coral reef**.

The island of Ireland.

ISTHMUS

An *isthmus* is a narrow strip of land that connects two larger areas of land that would otherwise be separated. An *isthmus* can be thought of as the land version of a **strait**. A **tombolo** is an *isthmus* that attaches an island to a mainland. It is formed from a **spit** or **shoal**. A **land bridge** is an *isthmus* that connects **Earth's** major landmasses. A **canal** may cut through the *isthmus* to create a shortcut for marine transport. An example of this is the Panama Canal.

LAGOON
A *lagoon* is a shallow body of water separated from a larger body of water by a **reef** or some sort of barrier such as a **spit**. The *lagoon* may be nearly or completely cut off from the larger body of water. An **atoll** is a ring shaped **coral reef** that partially or completely encircles a body of water, creating an atoll *lagoon*.

LAKE

A *lake* is a body of water within a **basin**, surrounded by land, apart from any inlet or outlet feeding or draining the *lake*, such as a **river** or **stream**. A *lake* is found inland, unlike the similar **lagoon**, which is found by the **sea** or **ocean**. A **pond** is smaller and more shallow than a *lake*. An artificial *lake* is called a **reservoir** and may be created for a source of electricity and water supply.

LANDFORM
A *landform* is any natural feature that appears on the solid surface of **Earth**.

▲ MARSH
A *marsh* is a type of **wetland** that is dominated by herbaceous (meaning non-wood) plants, such as reeds and tall grass. *Marshes* often occur close to **rivers** and **lakes**.

An Oxbow Lake

MEANDER

A *meander* is a large bend that occurs in a **river** or **stream**. A meander forms and grows when a small bend in a river or stream gets bigger due to river erosion on the outside and deposition on the inside. When the *meander* bends into itself, an **oxbow lake** is formed, and the **river** follows a more straight path.

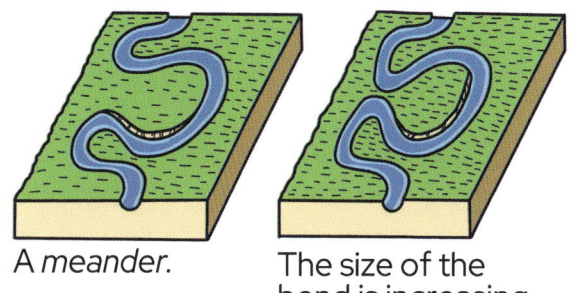

A *meander*. The size of the bend is increasing.

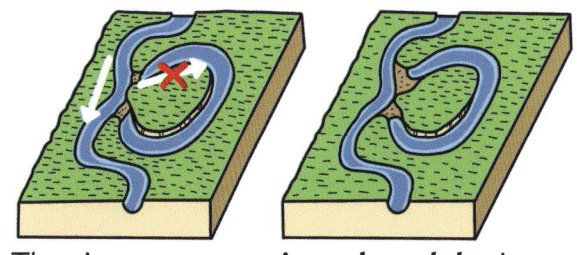

The river **channel** breaks through and water no longer flows around the bend.

An **oxbow lake** is formed.

MOUNTAIN

A *mountain* is an elevated part of Earth's surface that normally have steep sides and exposed rock. Most *mountains* are part of a **mountain range**, a chain of mountains that are connected by high ground, such as a **ridge**. A **hill** is a small *mountain* that is much less steep and less tall. The top of the *mountain* is called the **summit** or **peak**.

OASIS

An *oasis* is a fertile area in a **desert** or dry environment. It forms when an underground water source, such as an **aquifer**, surfaces or comes close to surfacing. This water source allows trees and other plants to grow. Surrounding the *oasis* in the picture are sand **dunes**, which are hills formed by the action of wind on sand.

OCEAN

An *ocean (also called sea in most cases)* is the body of salt water that makes up 71% of **Earth's** surface area. A **sea** is the same as an *ocean*, but it's meaning may be extended to mean portions of the *ocean* that are enclosed by land, such as the Mediterranean Sea. The five major *oceans* are the Pacific, Atlantic, Indian, Southern and Arctic.

PEATLAND

A *peatland (or mire, quagmire)* is a type of **wetland** dominated by **peat**-forming plants. **Peat** is the partial decomposition of plant material, forming a material that looks like wet mud. **Fens** and **bogs** are types of *peatland*. A **fen** is more alkaline than a **bog** (which is acidic) and therefore has more plants than a **bog**.

PENINSULA

A *peninsula* is land that is surrounded by a water on most sides apart from the land which it extends from. A **headland (or head)** is a *peninsula* that is usually high with steep slopes or **cliffs**. A **cape** is a larger **headland**. A **spit** is a sandy *peninsula* that has been formed by longshore drift.

The Florida peninsula, USA

PLAIN
A *plain* is an expanse of land that is generally flat. They are found close to **rivers**, where they are called **flood plains**. *Plains* also occur on top of **plateaus**, and in many **grassland** and **tundra** biomes.

PLATEAU

A *plateau* is a flat area of land, such as a **plain**, that is steeply raised from surrounding land on one or more sides. A *plateau* may also be called a **tableland**.

An **escarpment** or **scarp** is a long **cliff** that separates two flat grounds, giving them different elevations. An **escarpment** and *plateau* are often present together, the *plateau* referring to the flat higher ground and the **escarpment** referring to the **cliff** face.

RAINFOREST

A *rainforest* is a **forest** with large, continuous amounts of rainfall. *Rainforests* are either temperate or tropical. Tropical *rainforests*, such as the Amazon rainforest are hot all year round, but temperate *rainforests* are colder over the winter. *Rainforests* often have a canopy layer that blocks sunlight and prevents plants and smaller trees (often seen in **jungles**) from growing.

Jungles are thick and tangled trees that are seen alongside tropical *rainforests*. The main difference between them is that **jungles** have a lot of undergrowth (such as vines) that makes travelling through them difficult.

REEF

A *reef* is an underwater **ridge** or **shoal** of stable material such as rock or coral. *Reefs* may be formed from deposition of sand, wave erosion, or by coral, as in a **coral reef**. Most *reefs* remain underwater, but if they surface above water, they may create **atolls**, **cays**, **lagoons** and other **landforms**.

RIA

A *ria* is a coastal **inlet** and **bay** caused by the flooding of a **valley** by seawater. A *ria* is similar to a **sound** or an **estuary**. A *ria* is less narrow and has less steep sides than a **fiord**. A **harbor** (or **harbour**) is a sheltered body of water where ships can be docked, and because *rias* are coastal inlets and sheltered, they make good natural **harbors.** For example: Sydney Harbor.

RIDGE

A *ridge* is a feature in a **mountain range** where the land connecting the **mountains** is elevated. The resulting elevation forms a continuous crest. The lowest point of the *ridge* connecting **mountains** is called a **col**.

A **saddle** is an area along the *ridge* where the *ridge* on either side is directly higher. A **mountain pass** is a navigable route over a *ridge* or **mountain range**. **Saddles**, being the low area of a *ridge*, make them common places for a **mountain pass**.

RIVER

A *river* is a natural, flowing course of water. The apparent start of the *river* is called the **source (or river source)**, which is often a **spring**. A *river* generally flows towards another body of water, such as an **ocean**, **sea** or **lake**. A **stream** and **creek** is a small *river*. A **rapid** is a part of the *river* with a steep gradient and increased speed.

SALT PAN
A *salt pan (or salt flat)* is a flat expanse with covered with salt. They form when a body of water such as a **lake** evaporates. *Salt pans* are mostly found in **deserts**.

SAVANNA
A *savanna (also spelt savannah)* is a mixed **woodland-grassland biome** where trees are common but spaced far enough from each other to allow sunlight to reach the ground and support the growth of grass. *Savannas* are often tropical, and experience seasonal rain. *Savannas* appear between **desert** and **forest** or **grassland biomes**.

SHOAL

A *shoal* is an underwater **ridge, sandbank or sandbar** that rises from the bottom of the body of water to near - or above - the surface. *Shoals* are also called **sandbanks** or **sandbars**. A *shoal* is formed from underwater currents.

▲SPIT

A *spit* is a **shoal** and a type of **peninsula** that has been formed due to the deposition of material (often sand) from waves in a process called longshore drift. Longshore drift transports material down a **beach** and past the end, creating a *spit* that sticks out from the surrounding **beach**. If the *spit* attaches an **island**, then it is called a **tombolo**.

▲SPRING

A *spring* is a point where water flows from an underground water store called an **aquifer**, to **Earth's** surface. **Springs** are common **river sources**.

▲STEPPE

A *steppe* is a large region of **grassland plain** where trees are uncommon. A **prairie** is a type of *steppe* that originates in North America. *Steppes* are too dry to support **forests** but not dry enough to be a **desert**.

SWAMP

A *swamp* is a type of **wetland** that is dominated by **forest** or wooded plants. *Swamps* often occur close to **rivers** and **lakes**.

TAIGA

A *taiga* is a **biome** consisting of abundant coniferous **forests.** The trees are often evergreen, meaning the leaves remain green throughout the year, and include pines and spruces. *Taiga* is also called **snow forests** or **boreal forests**. *Taigas* often have extreme climates that consist of very cold, long winters and short, warm summers.

TUNDRA

A *tundra* is a **biome** where trees do not grow because of the low temperatures. A *tundra* landscape is normally bare, with only small shrubs, grass, lichen and mosses growing. Underground soil in *tundras* are often frozen permanently; this is called **permafrost**. A *tundra* by it's climatic definition is a region where no month sees average temperatures above 10°C / 50°F.

VALLEY

A *valley* is a long, low area surrounded by **hills** or **mountains**. Often, a *valley* will have a **river** or **stream** flowing from one end to the other. Most *valleys* are created by erosion from the **river** or **stream** over long periods of time. **Canyons** and **gorges** are both types of *valley*, specifically a narrow *valley* surrounded by steep, rocky **cliff** faces.

VOLCANO

A *volcano* is a rupture on **Earth's** crust that allows **lava**, ash and gases to escape from a **magma chamber** below. *Volcanoes* are a result of tectonic activity, mainly from where tectonic plates, that form **Earth's** crust, crash into each other (converge) or move apart (diverge). After an eruption, a *volcano* may form a circular **depression** called a volcanic **crater**. If the eruption is large enough to empty the **magma chamber**, then a **caldera** may form.

Lava and **magma** both mean molten rock, **lava** specifically meaning molten rock found on **Earth's** surface, and **magma** is molten rock inside of **Earth**.

WATERFALL

A *waterfall* is where flowing water, such as a **river** or **stream**, flows over a vertical drop or several vertical drops. The vertical drop can also be a **cliff**, as shown in the picture. Water from the *waterfall* drops into a **plunge pool**, a deep pool at the bottom of the *waterfall*. Both a *waterfall* and **plunge pool** are formed by erosion of the flowing water over time.

WETLAND

A *wetland* is an area of land that is flooded by water, giving rise to a **biome** with unique vegetation. *Wetlands* often occur as a transition zone between a body of water, such as a **river**, and land. There are several main types of *wetlands*, including **marshes**, **swamps** and **peatlands**.

INDEX

affluent 15
aquifer 43
arch 3
archipelago 4
arete 38
atoll 24

badlands 7
bar 42
basin 13
bay 5
beach 6
bight 5
biome 7
bluff 11
bog 31
boreal forest 45
butte 7

caldera 13, 48
canal 10
canyon 8, 47
cape 32
cave 9
cavern 9
cay 22
channel 10
cliff 11
coast 6
col 38
column 9
confluence 15
continent 12
coral reef 36
cove 5
crater 48
creek 39
crevasse 20

delta 12
depression 13

desert 14
distributaries 12
drainage basin ... 15
drainage divide . 15
dunes 14, 29

earth 16
equator 16
escarpment .. 7, 34
estuary 17

fen 31
fiord / fjord 18
forest 18

geyser 19
glacier 20
globe 16
gorge 8, 47
grassland 21
gulf 5
gully 8

harbor 37
head 32
headland 32
hill 21, 28
hillock 7

ice sheet 20
iceberg 20
inlet 5
island 22
isle 22
islet 22
isthmus 23

jungle 35

key 22
knoll 7

lagoon 24
lake 25

land bridge 23
landform 26
lava 48

magma 48
magma chamber 48
marsh 26
meander 27
mesa 7
mire 31
moraine 20
mountain 28
mountain pass 38
mountain range . 28

north pole 16

oasis 14, 29
ocean 30
oxbow lake 27

peak 28
peatland 31
peninsula 32
permafrost 46
plain 33
plateau 34
plunge pool 49
pond 25
polar desert 14
prairie 43

rainforest 35
rapids 39
ravine 8
reef 36
reservoir 25
ria 37
ridge 38
river 39
river source 39

saddle 38
salt flat 40

salt pan 40
sandbank 42
sandbar 42
savanna/savannah .. 41
scarp 34
sea 5, 30
sea arch 3
sea stack 3
seashore 6
shoal 42
shore 6
sinkhole 13
snow forest 45
sound 18
source 39
south pole 16
spit 32, 42
spring 43
stack 3
stalactite 9
stalagmite 9
strait 10
stream 39
steppe 43
summit 28
swamp 44

tableland 34
taiga 45
tombolo 23, 42
tributary 15
tropic of cancer 16
tropic of capricorn .. 16
tundra 46

valley 13, 47
volcano 48

waterfall 49
watershed 15
wetland 49
woodland 19

Printed in Great Britain
by Amazon